W9-AKC-235

I Have Enough Stuff

by Connie Beyer Horn

Illustrated by Chris Sharp and Gary Currant

Concordia Publishing House

To mother:
She taught us that with love and
laughter we had enough.

Copyright © 1998 Concordia Publishing House
3558 S. Jefferson Avenue, St. Louis, MO 63118-3968
Manufactured in U.S.A.

2 3 4 5 6 7 8 9 10   07 06 05 04 03 02 01

Dear Parent/Teacher,

Throughout our lives we accumulate things; some precious, some pretty, some large, and some small. This book paints images of the collections of children, teaching in the process that all things are subject to loss or change. All things, of course, except the love and care of our Lord Jesus Christ.

As you read this book, allow it to remind you and your child that as long as we have Jesus as our Savior, we have all we really need.

Connie Beyer Horn

I have a kite with colored string,
And a baseball bat to swing,
And a bird that likes to sing.

I have a lizard and some frogs,
And a kitten and two dogs,
And a fort made out of logs,
  And a kite with colored string,
  And a baseball bat to swing,
  And a bird that likes to sing.

I have three arrows and a bow,
And a flute that I can blow,
And some mittens for the snow,
   And a lizard and some frogs,
   And kitten and two dogs,
   And a fort made out of logs,
      And a kite with colored string,
      And a baseball bat to swing,
      And a bird that likes to sing.

I have Jesus as my Friend,
And my soul He saved from sin,
And His love will never end!

And three arrows and a bow,
And a flute that I can blow,
And some mittens for the snow,
　　And a lizard and some frogs,
　　And a kitten and two dogs,
　　And a fort made out of logs,
　　　And a kite with colored string,
　　　And a baseball bat to swing,
　　　And a bird that likes to sing.

Is that enough stuff?

But my kite crashed in a tree,
And I struck out one—two—three—,
And my bird just looks at me.

But I still have enough stuff.

I have a lizard and some frogs,
And a kitten and two dogs,
And a fort made out of logs.
   I have three arrows and a bow,
   And a flute that I can blow,
   And some mittens for the snow.
      I have Jesus as my Friend,
      And my soul He saved from sin,
      And His love will never end!

Yes, I have enough.

But my lizard and the frogs,
Ran away from those two dogs.
And my kitten's now a cat,
Eating well and getting fat.
And the logs that made my fort,
Fit me best when I was short.
And my kite crashed in a tree,
And I struck out one—two—three—,
And my bird just looks at me.

But I have enough stuff.

I have three arrows and a bow,
And a flute that I can blow,
And some mittens for the snow.
 I have Jesus as my Friend,
 And my soul He saved from sin,
 And His love will never end!

Now my arrows have been lost,
And the flute my father tossed,
And my mittens let in frost.
And the lizard and the frogs,
Ran away from those two dogs.
And my kitten's now a cat,
Eating well and getting fat.
And the logs that made a fort,
Fit me best when I was short.
And my kite crashed in a tree,
And I struck out one—
two—three—,
And my bird just looks
at me.

But I still have enough stuff.

I have Jesus as my Friend,
And my soul He saved from sin,
And His love will never end!

Yes, I have enough.

Though my arrows may be lost,
And the flute my father tossed,
And my mittens let in frost,
And the lizard and the frogs,
Ran away from those two dogs,
And my kitten's now a cat,
Eating well and getting fat,
And the logs that made my fort,
Fit me best when I was short,
And my kite crashed in a tree,
And I struck out one—two—three—,
And my bird just looks at me,

I still have enough stuff.

I have Jesus as my Friend,
And my soul He saved from sin,
And His love will never end!

Yes, I have enough!

Draw a picture of you and your friends with Jesus.